/

12 Ways Forgiveness Will Change Everything

12 Ways Forgiveness Will Change Everything

because everybody really does need to forgive somebody

DR. ALLEN HUNT

wellspring

Cover and Interior Design: Todd Detering

ISBN: 978-1-63582-260-1 (hardcover)
ISBN: 978-1-63582-530-5 (eBook)

Printed in the United States of America.

10   9   8   7   6   5   4   3   2   1

To Wayne, Freddie, Ken, and Fred
Great Teachers

| TABLE OF CONTENTS |

Prologue: The Ultimate Power Tool 1

Introduction: The Promise 7

1   Know Who You Are: Mother Emanuel 11

2   Master the Little Things: Teresa 17

3   Draw Near to Forgivers: Wounded Warrior 25

4   Own Your Attitude: A Rabbi and a Priest 31

5   Accept the Invitation: Dismas 37

6   Forgive Yourself: Ron 43

7   Taste the Sweetness: Dominic 51

8   Past the Hurt: Wanda 57

9   Reach Out: Nina 63

10 Resurrection Faith: Melissa 69

11 The Air You Breathe: The Amish 79

12 Heroic Love: Leonella 87

Closing Word: Today Is Your Day 93

About the Author 97

Discussion Guide 99

The Ultimate Power Tool

I met Brian at the hardware store, where he works selling power tools. He helped me select a blower.

After the purchase, I then invited the manager of the store, a friend of mine, to lunch. We asked Brian to join us.

"Sure!" Brian replied. "Wait a minute, and let me grab my stuff." He scampered into the back room of the store and reemerged holding an overstuffed duffel bag.

Getting into the car, he plopped that carryall on the back seat. When we arrived at the restaurant, he toted his bag in and carefully placed it on the seat next to him.

I had to ask him: The curiosity was killing me.

"Brian, I'm glad you could join us. But I gotta know: What's with the duffel bag?"

He unzipped it. And out came a collection of notebooks and file folders.

"I take these with me everywhere I go," he said. "I don't want to lose them."

"What are they?" I asked.

He flipped through a notebook. His eyes focused intently on the pages. "I keep a record of everyone who's done me wrong—cheated me, lied to me, taken what's mine. I've written it all down right here. I keep these wrongs with me so I can remember them all."

That catalog of injustices accompanies Brian everywhere he goes. Everywhere. All the time. The weight grows each day as he adds names and grudges to his files: his personal attempt to make sense of a world where we wound one another every day.

From the looks of that jam-packed bag, he will soon have to buy a second one. Or maybe even upgrade to a wheelbarrow to make room for all the insults in his life. Because they just keep accumulating. At work. At home. Even at lunch with me, perhaps. Yikes!

Maybe he should digitize his records. That would lighten the physical load, although I suppose it wouldn't relieve the emotional load Brian carries.

I wish he knew that clinging to all those grudges will kill him. Like a ship unable to set sail, held back by an anchor of old wounds. No voyage. No destination. No future.

The truth is very simple: Bitterness and resentment slowly destroy your heart from the inside out.

Unless you do something about it.

Let's face it, our culture has grown toxic. Social media has transformed gossip into a big-money business.

We love to sit on the couch, eating a bag of Cheetos and chugging a Mountain Dew while spewing opinions as fast as we can. We post opinions about other people's lives. Opinions about their decisions, especially their mistakes. Opinions about politicians, about celebrities, about leaders—anybody at all, really.

Social media has even made it easier for us to destroy complete strangers. And to do it with vengeful delight: a tweet here, a Facebook comment there. Some folks like to call it venting, but it's really just gossip—or slander. We spread harmful words to or about anyone we disagree with or dislike. All in a vain effort to feel better about ourselves or our own group.

It's like a little voice inside us says to other people online, "I may not know you, but I hate you. I hate your group and your affiliations. So I'm going to crush you."

All the while we convince ourselves that somehow our posts are making us feel better, or even making the world better.

Advertisers and social media billionaires love it. They rake in the dough, enticing us to hate and to gossip with ever more venom. Gossip is profitable. It's easy. And it's cheap.

Even worse, you and I live in a culture that likes to pile on people at their lowest moments. We rush to judge a person by a single mistake. Our culture values yelling more than listening. Cancellation more than kindness. Destruction more than mercy.

It's as if we really believe a person can't change or grow. Make a mistake around here and you're finished. Mistake-makers must be punished swiftly and severely. Or better yet, eliminated. Canceled. Forever.

But you and I know differently.

When we swim in the toxic waters of bitterness, we'll drown. We weren't made for those seas. We weren't made for condemnation and gossip. You and I were made for greatness. Most of all, we were made for an ocean of love.

Deep down, we know there's a different way. A path that leads to healing. To second chances. To growth. And, yes, to redemption.

That way is forgiveness.

Two Jewish men survived the Holocaust together. They suffered, endured, and lived through to the other side. And then they went their separate ways.

Thirty years later, both men were invited to give a presentation at a school. To reunite and share what they had lived through.

At the presentation, they were asked, "Have you forgiven the Nazis for what they did to you and your families?"

The first man responded, "Never! I'll never let those bastards off the hook. They were evil. I will never forget. And I'll never forgive them!"

The second man replied, "Yes. I have forgiven them. I had no choice but to forgive so I could move on with my life."

The first man screamed at him angrily, "How dare you forgive those evil bastards? How could you?!"

The second man gently said, "How sad I am for you, that after all these years, you are still owned by the Nazis. How sad I am that they still imprison your mind."

The truth is simple: You have a choice.

You can collect and cling to the many hurts and wounds of your life. You can even carry them around with you everywhere you go—perhaps in a duffel bag or simply in your heart.

Or.

You can forgive. You can choose to release the pain. You can simply refuse to carry the poison of anger, bitterness, even hatred inside you. You can choose to be free from the prison of hate.

The choice is yours.

I will tell you this: When you're facing death, you will quickly discover how much time you've wasted in life holding grudges and being angry for no good reason. In fact, you'll find yourself saying, "I wish I'd just let it all go and chosen to be happy instead."

Forgiveness unleashes power in your life. It's the ultimate power tool. But it's usually underrated and often ignored. Yet that power stands waiting, ready to transform your life right now. To free you from the hurts of the past. So you can step into a bigger and brighter future. To release the poison of resentment inside you. So you can be filled with hope and joy instead.

The world needs the power of forgiveness today more than ever before.

That's why I've written this book. Because everybody *really* does need to forgive somebody.

The Promise

"Forgiving isn't something you do for someone else.
It's something you do for yourself. It's saying, 'You're not
important enough to have a stranglehold on me.'"
— Jodi Picoult —

Who's your Somebody?

Everybody needs to forgive somebody.

So, who's yours? Who do you need to forgive?

We all have one. Perhaps you have more. But for right now, focus only on one. The person you most need to forgive. Maybe it's the teacher who humiliated you in front of the entire class. Or perhaps it's your ex-spouse who violated your vows and destroyed your marriage. Or it might be your mother or father, whose alcoholism drove a wedge into your family and nearly crushed your spirit. Or the person you most need to forgive may actually be yourself.

You know the one you need to forgive. That's your Somebody. Bring that person's face into your mind. This might be painful for you—how can you possibly forgive that deep, deep hurt?

As we begin this journey, just know God has more in store for you than you can possibly imagine.

Some people seem to be naturally good forgivers. Maybe they're born that way. But most of us have to learn how to forgive. How can that happen?

Do you slowly learn how to forgive over time?

Can you get better with practice? Possibly develop a mercy muscle much like you do by working out your body with weights?

Will consistent inspiration from books and stories make you a great forgiver?

Is your own ability to forgive perhaps the result of you yourself having been forgiven by someone else?

Does the family you grow up in shape how well you forgive?

Can you forgive through sheer willpower once you realize you're carrying a bitterness that will kill you unless you learn to let it go?

The answer to all these questions is yes. They're all true. All at the same time.

I've found this to be the case in my three decades of studying forgiveness, in my coaching of others—and in learning how to forgive in my own life.

Because, let's be real: Forgiveness is hard.

You may well discover that forgiveness more often is a journey rather than a destination. For example, you might have to forgive someone over and over again for the same hurt.

Let's say your father hurt you when you were a child. You work to forgive him when you are young. Years later, you get married. This big change in your life reminds you of your father's actions years ago, and you find you need to forgive him again. Then you become a father. When you look at your own child, it triggers the reemergence of memories from your childhood. And you realize you need to forgive your own father once more for that old pain you still carry. Finally, when your father approaches his own death, you walk alongside him to help him finish life well. And you discover again that old wound from your childhood still leaves a residue in your heart. So you choose to forgive him yet again.

Forgiveness is hard. And it can take time.

This book will help.

First, it will give you inspiration to believe you can forgive.

Then it *will* provide you real tools so you will forgive.

I have filled this book with ordinary stories of forgiveness to help you. All of the stories are true. They will remind you that you too can forgive.

But I've also included a few extraordinary, almost miraculous stories. To paint a picture of the amazing possibilities forgiveness can create in your life.

Most of these stories come from other people rather than from me. Real people who have something to teach you and me about how to live. And about how to reject a cold-blooded culture of cruel condemnation.

Once you've heard their stories, you will be the better for it. And when you become better, the world becomes better too. It starts and ends with you.

After each story, I also share a real-life coaching tip. These tips, just like the stories themselves, will help you forgive your Somebody. Be honest: What have you got to lose? A few resentments? Some bitterness?

Embrace the inspiration and tools here in this book.

When you do, you'll be one step closer to becoming just who God made you to be. And you'll be healthier and happier than ever before.

CHAPTER 1

Know Who You Are: Mother Emanuel

"As far as the east is from the west,
so far does he remove our transgressions from us."
— Psalm 103:12 —

Miracle.

There's no other word for it.

Miracle. As in, other-worldly, supernatural, not explainable with mere words.

That's what happened when amazing grace pierced the heart of every listener in a drab courtroom. At the bail hearing for a young white man, Dylann Roof, in Charleston, South Carolina, accused (and later convicted) of murdering nine African Americans. All of whom were attending a Bible study at Mother Emanuel A.M.E. Church.

Family members of the nine victims spoke spontaneously to

the court and to the murderer. Their unscripted words flowed like water spouting from never-ending springs. And should have earned them the Nobel Peace Prize.

For example, hear the heart of Nadine Collier, whose mother, Ethel, was killed: "I forgive you. You took something very precious away from me. I will never get to talk to her ever again. I will never be able to hold her again, but I forgive you. . . You hurt me. You hurt a lot of people. But if God forgives you, I forgive you."

Alana Simmons, whose grandfather, Daniel, was killed, didn't plan to speak at the hearing but found herself inspired by Ms. Collier. "We are here to combat hate-filled actions with love-filled actions," she said.

Christians are used to being mocked as stupid or hypocritical. We often just laugh along with the joke. But these public statements laid out the very heart of the faith, pure and beautiful.

Hearing the words of these people suffering the worst imaginable losses, you couldn't just dismiss them. You could only feel amazement and ask yourself: "If I were in that situation, would I be great too?"

Nadine Collier became famous for the three words she said to Dylann Roof: "I forgive you."

She learned in that bond hearing that forgiveness isn't weakness. It's not a duty done begrudgingly.

Forgiveness is free, but it's not cheap. Ms. Collier is trying to move on. She misses the sound of her mother's voice, the smile on her face as she greeted worshipers at church, the spring in her step when she moved forward to receive Communion.

But Collier's words, spoken just two days after the massacre, still hang powerfully in the air, all these years later: "I forgive you."

That's what her mother would have wanted, she says. "I know she would have said, 'That's my baby. I taught her well.'

"Forgiveness is power," she declares. "It means you can fight everything and anything head-on."

Today, the home the Rev. Anthony Thompson shared with his wife, Myra, who was leading the Bible study that night, seems too quiet. Reminders of Myra stand everywhere: fresh flowers on the table, just the way she liked them; a photo of her on the wall; her Bible, with the text marked for that night, along with her notes from the Bible study.

When Rev. Thompson last saw her, just before she left, Myra seemed to glow, he said. As if everything were right in the world. Then she glided out the door before he had a chance to say goodbye.

He hadn't planned on attending the bond hearing at first. But something nudged him to go. In the courtroom, he felt God speak to him, telling him to forgive Dylann Roof.

After the hearing, Thompson felt a sense of serenity. "Later

I said: 'Oh my gosh, that was for my kids, and me, so we could have peace."

Life was hard after the murders for Bethane Middleton-Brown, whose sister, DePayne, left behind four children. Brown, and her husband, Antonio, raised them, along with the couple's own three children. She refused to hate Dylann Roof, however, and said her sister would have wanted her to forgive him.

Middleton-Brown, who passed away in March 2021, said of her murdered sister: "She taught me that we're the family love built. We have no room for hating, so we have to forgive."

In other words, Bethane Middleton-Brown knew who she was before she even entered that courtroom: a person of love. A forgiver.

She described her sister as a generous person, always ready to give, even though she never had much money. What she had in abundance was love and faith.

"God is taking me to a higher level," Ms. Middleton-Brown said. "If the man who killed my sister was looking for hate— he came to the wrong place."

The world often thinks progress depends on anger, aggression, and protesting. But on that day in Charleston, every American saw anger lose to love.

Forgiveness wins.

Miracle—there's just no other word for it.

FORGIVENESS COACHING TIP 1:
Know Who You Are

Forgiving is more about who you are than what you do. It's about who you are deep down inside. Who you see yourself as. Who you hope to become.

Nadine Collier and Bethane Middleton-Brown knew who they were. Forgivers. People of love. That identity defined them and guided their words in the moment they stood before the man who murdered their loved ones.

Decide today to begin to forgive your Somebody. Not because of who they are. But because of who you are.

It may take some time. Hard work. Maybe even some discomfort.

But you can do this. Because you know who you are.

Say these words out loud: "I am a forgiver. I will choose grace."

This is your identity. And your destiny.

I am a forgiver. I will choose grace.

CHAPTER 2

Master the Little Things: Teresa

"Blessed are the pure in heart, for they shall see God."
— Jesus —

People really can get on your nerves.

Your co-worker may have an irritating habit, like interrupting you every time you speak. Or maybe your brother annoys you with his obsessive need to be the first one to order anytime you're at a restaurant. Or perhaps your friend steps on your last nerve when she tells you the exact same story for the forty-third time.

People are mostly human. You know that. And each one of us is wonderfully imperfect. Perfectly imperfect, actually.

We each do little things that annoy the people around us. We make small mistakes when we're careless. We can do a dozen thoughtless things a day. Because we are human. Perfectly imperfect.

We first learn to forgive by forgiving the little things. It's just like learning to walk before running. And learning to climb stairs before climbing Mount Everest.

Before we can be capable of forgiving the deepest of wounds, we need to master forgiving the little things: the petty annoyances and irritating habits of the people around us. When we become good at forgiving these little things, it becomes much easier to forgive the larger wounds and disappointments that will inevitably arrive.

There's also a very good reason to learn to forgive the little things: if you're not careful, tiny annoyances can build up inside you like a pressure cooker, until one day either

a.) You explode in volcanic anger from all the petty grievances crammed tightly inside you

Or

b.) You find yourself completely unable to be around someone because they irritate you so much.

What to do?

Teresa found a powerful way to forgive the little things.

She lived in a large house with a group of women. These women did virtually everything together. They worked together. They prayed together. They laughed and cried together. They ate together. And all that togetherness was just a whole lot of, well, together!

When you spend that much time with the same people in the same space, it's almost inevitable that one of those people will begin to get on your nerves. Any wife will tell you that about her husband. Maybe it's his annoying habit of leaving the dirty clothes in the middle of the floor or clipping his fingernails while sitting in bed. Day in and day out, a little annoyance can burn inside you like a fuse on a stick of dynamite. The little things build up and become big things. They will make your skin crawl, your mind race, your temper burn... if you don't learn to forgive the simple things.

So Teresa found a solution to her situation. In her community of women, she had one colleague who simply got on her nerves every day, whenever they were together. Here, in her own words, is how Teresa learned to forgive the little things:

*There is in the community a sister who has the faculty of displeasing me in everything, in her ways, her words, her character, everything seems very disagreeable to me. And still, she. . . must be very pleasing to God. Not wishing to give in to the natural antipathy I was experiencing, I told myself that charity must not consist in feelings but in works; then **I set myself to doing for this sister what I would do for the person I loved the most. Each time I met her I prayed to God for her, offering him all the virtues and merits.** [emphasis added]*

I felt this was pleasing to Jesus, for there is no artist who doesn't love to receive praise for His works, and Jesus, the artist of souls, is happy when. . . we admire its beauty. I wasn't content simply with praying very much for this sister who gave me so many struggles, **but I took care to render her all the services possible...** *[emphasis added]*

One day at recreation she asked in almost these words: "Would you tell me, Sister Therese. . . what attracts you so much toward me; every time you look at me, I see you smile?" *[emphasis added]*

Ahhh! What attracted me was Jesus hidden in the depths of her soul; Jesus who makes sweet what is most bitter. I answered that I was smiling because I was happy to see her. *[emphasis added]*

How did Teresa do it? She turned the tables. Instead of little annoyances to be harbored, she discovered little opportunities to serve her religious sister.

Teresa began to imagine that the sister who annoyed her was the person she actually loved the most. And she began to act accordingly. She not only prayed for her, she served her. As generously and kindly as she could.

She smiled rather than winced each time she met her. She said a prayer of gratitude when she saw her. She served her with gladness when the opportunity presented itself.

In short, Teresa turned her irritation into action. She learned to move from petty annoyance to humble love. Forgiveness then became easy. And Teresa mastered the little things.

You remember the story. Jesus and His disciples are walking along the side of the road. Peter comes up and says, "Hey Jesus, if one of my brothers hurts me, how many times do I have to forgive him? Seven?"

Peter swells with pride, impressed with himself at the thought of forgiving someone seven times for the same thing. After all, that's a lot of forgiving.

Jesus responds carefully. You can almost see Him looking inward, into His own heart of grace. He looks at Peter and says, "No. Not seven. Try seventy times seven."

Seventy times seven? Four hundred ninety times? Really?! Wow. Jesus is an extremist.

It's unpopular to say. It's insensitive even to consider. But yes, when it comes to forgiveness, Jesus is an extremist.

You and I desperately need to hear that.

Put down your duffel bag full of grudges and insecurities. Put down your desire to pronounce judgment on other people. And forgive.

It works. Married couples often tend to fixate on each other's minor flaws or annoying habits. The little things that drive your spouse crazy because they happen day after day after day. The wife obsesses about her husband's messiness or the husband fixates on his wife's forgetfulness.

One study encouraged couples to create a gratitude journal, in which they were to write down three things each day about their spouse that they were grateful for. The purpose was to turn their attention from irritation to gratitude, in the littlest of things.

When they intentionally focused on gratitude, eight out of ten couples experienced significant improvement in their marriages. They moved from petty annoyances and "You're so on my nerves!" to finding appreciation and love. The simple act of writing your gratitude can turn the tables. It works for marriages. And it will work for you.

It's all about the little things. And those little things fade away when you make the conscious decision to be grateful and serve someone rather than obsess and fixate on their flaws.

Maybe that's why Teresa became St. Therese of Lisieux. She discovered that the secret to the big things is to consistently master the little things.

FORGIVENESS COACHING TIP 2:
Start Small

Teresa discovered the nuclear power of little things. When a roommate or colleague annoyed her, she changed the spirit of the relationship from irritation to love. By offering a smile. A kind word. A thoughtful touch. A word offered to God.

Name a person who annoys you. Feel free to write his or her name in the margin of the page right here.

Now, close your eyes and envision that person in your mind's eye. Begin to see them not as an annoyance but as a person you can begin to practice forgiveness on.

Are there ways you can serve that person with humble love? Are you able to turn your irritation into healing action?

Rather than allowing him or her to live on your last nerve with an annoying habit, can you see an opportunity to change the spirit of the relationship by doing little things just like Teresa did?

When you can do that, you will have begun to master the little things. And you will start making your way to higher levels of forgiveness.

CHAPTER 3

Draw Near to Forgivers: Wounded Warrior

*"The ordinary acts we practice every day at home are of more
importance to the soul than their simplicity might suggest."*
— Thomas Moore —

I love Lourdes, France. It's a place unlike any other.

The scenic beauty of the French mountains.

The quaint intimate village.

The grotto where Mary appeared to Bernadette.

And the healing that has emerged through the miraculous
waters flowing there.

Most of all, I love the crowds. People come from all
around the world, making their way to Lourdes seeking the
healing balm of sacred water. Hoping to bathe in the waters
of Mary.

The crowds inspire you when you are really paying attention. Children in wheelchairs. The elderly limping. The
disfigured hoping. The disabled using any means possible

to find their way to the baths—even the bedridden, being pushed on gurneys by volunteers, servants smiling as they share the love of God and the mercy of Mary.

All God's children. Every flavor. Every shape. Every tongue. Banded together in the hope of encountering Christ Jesus. And finding healing for their burdens.

People come to Lourdes for healing.

You never know the burdens people carry. Some physical. Some emotional. Each one unique. Each one deeply personal.

Lourdes is a special place. The rock walls of the grotto there are completely smooth. Made that way by millions of pilgrims prayerfully pressing their palms to the stone. In tears. In grace. In hope.

I read about one priest who journeyed with an ill friend for eight days to seek the powerful waters in Lourdes.

During that pilgrimage, the priest met a young man who had no legs. Later, the group shared a foot-washing experience. The priest watched as a woman knelt before the young man. Rather than washing his feet, she gently washed, dried, and kissed his stumps. His body had been maimed by a roadside bomb in Afghanistan. Like every pilgrim, he had come seeking hope and healing.

The man had come with his brother. The priest approached the brother and quietly thanked him for bringing the injured man to Lourdes.

The brother replied, "I didn't bring him. He brought me. He's accepted what happened to him. I am the one full of bitterness and hate."

Heavy words.

Forgiving the people who harm you is one thing. That takes courage and grace.

But forgiving the people who harm the ones you love can be another thing altogether. Forgiving the bully who intimidates your child. Or the in-law who degrades your sister. Or the boss who fires your husband. Now that can be tough.

Yet the wounded soldier, maimed for life by someone he'd never met, came to accept and forgive. And in turn he offered a place of peace to his brother, whose own deep injury came from watching his beloved sibling suffer.

Sometimes forgiveness is contagious, like a virus transmitted by inhaling the breath of a nearby person. In the same way, forgiveness can often come from drawing near to someone who has already forgiven and inhaling that grace.

The wounded young man didn't waste his pain. He recycled it into healing and offered it to his brother.

Like the brother, when you struggle to forgive, draw near to someone who's a good forgiver. Breathe in their breath. Inhale the grace.

When you have forgiven a great wrong in your life, don't keep that healing to yourself. Recycle it and offer the resulting grace to the people all around you.

The world will be glad you did.

FORGIVENESS COACHING TIP 3:
A Great Place to Start

The wounded soldier forgave his Somebody: the anonymous terrorist who planted the bomb on the side of the road.

But the soldier's brother was still struggling to forgive. He hoped to benefit simply by being near his brother and inhaling the grace that had changed his brother's bitterness into merciful acceptance.

It's OK if you can't forgive right now. Just find yourself some forgivers and spend time with them. That's a great place to start.

CHAPTER 4

Own Your Attitude:
A Rabbi and a Priest

*"Put aside your hatred and animosity. . . Pardon one another
so that later on you will not remember the injury. The recollection
of an injury. . . adds to our anger, nurtures our sin, and hates what is
good. It is a rusty arrow and poison for the soul. . . It is like
a worm in the mind. . . It remains planted in the soul like a nail. . .
It is indeed a daily death. . ."*
— Francis of Paola —

For a time, I served as a volunteer at a homeless shelter for families in a church. I gave one night each week. Helping serve the evening meal to the twelve families living in the church's indoor recreation space. Then visiting with them for a few hours simply to listen and offer encouragement as they struggled to stabilize their lives.

The shelter provided a safe place for those dozen families. Each family consisted of a father and mother living together with children. That was a requirement. The expectation was that one or both parents had a job of some kind or was actively seeking one.

The church asked us volunteers to meet once a week as a group. We would discuss what we were learning and experiencing and find ways to be more hospitable and helpful for the families. Our group often was led by Fr. Chet, the priest who led the congregation.

In our first meeting, I expressed my skepticism about whether some of these families actually deserved our help. I suspected that two of them were not particularly active in trying to find a job and that one of them was lying to us in all kinds of ways, in order to get a free, clean place to live.

"I don't believe these two families really deserve our help. How do we know we're not being taken advantage of?" I asked.

Fr. Chet calmly listened to my sanctimonious anger.

He then kindly looked at me and said to the group, "Allen, you may be right. But I know for sure I'd rather be called a sucker than called coldhearted."

The truth arrow pierced my heart. And punctured my self-righteousness.

I realized I couldn't control everyone else; I could only control me. And I was called to help people in the name of Jesus, whether or not I knew beyond a shadow of a doubt that they met my standards for deserving it. My role is not to hold God's clipboard and evaluate everyone on His behalf.

I couldn't control them, but I could control my own heart. I needed to own my attitude.

In an old Jewish story, a man comes to a rabbi to ask for help.

"I'm sick and I can't work," the man says. "My wife is ill too. She can't even take in laundry to make a little money. Even our children are unwell. I don't know what to do. Could you possibly give us a little help, just to tide us over?"

The rabbi reaches into his desk drawer, pulls out some money, and hands it to the struggling man.

That afternoon, a woman comes running to the rabbi and says, "Rabbi, you know the man who came to you this morning with that story about him being sick and his wife being sick and his children being sick too? Well, it's not true. None of them are sick!"

Hearing this, the rabbi exclaims joyfully, "Thank God they're all healthy!"

Be honest. If you had been in that rabbi's position, would that have been your immediate response? Or would you have felt cheated?

Now ask yourself which is more important—a hundred dollars, or the health of a family. Your faith almost certainly inspires you to reply the health of a family, right?

Here's the point. You can't control the people around you or their actions. You can, however, control you—and your response to any situation.

You can choose your attitude.

For example, if you were in a car accident today, you could respond by saying:

"I'm so mad I got in that accident. It made me late to work, and it's going to cost me a fortune to get my car repaired. I'm finding a lawyer!"

Or.

"I'm so glad I wasn't injured in that accident and no one else was seriously hurt."

You get to choose: anger or gratitude. It's entirely up to you.

You can't control everyone—or even anyone—else. But you can control you.

FORGIVENESS COACHING TIP 4:
Surround Yourself with Inspiration

Own a healthy attitude by surrounding yourself with motivating reminders to boost your attitude. And to inspire you to act on your best hopes.

One way to do that is to place powerful quotes nearby you for each part of your day: in your bedroom for when you wake up, in your kitchen for when you eat breakfast, in your car for your travel time, and in your office for your work or school hours.

Gather quotes that inspire you. Like the ones included between the chapters in this book. Write them down on a card or even a poster. After Fr. Chet spoke truth to me, I wrote his words down: "I'd rather be called a sucker than called coldhearted." And I still have them on my desk.

When you consider the Somebody you need to forgive, allow these quotes to call you to a higher place. When your mind wanders into a bad neighborhood of bitterness, let inspiring words help you focus on the good that is in you. And the healing joy you are seeking.

Inspire your path to forgiveness. Choose gratitude, not anger.

| CHAPTER 5 |

Accept the Invitation: Dismas

"Forgiveness is not an occasional act; it is a permanent attitude."
— Martin Luther King Jr. —

Imagine.

You're walking around town. Doing a little shopping here. Grabbing a cup of coffee there. It's afternoon. The sun is shining. It's a beautiful day.

You stumble upon a crowd, just on the edge of town. On a hillside.

Lots of people are gathered together. You hear shouts, cries, maybe even a little music rising from the crowd. Your curiosity is piqued. So you walk closer to see what's going on.

As you get to the hill, you find three tall crosses arranged in a row. Each has a man hanging from it. Nailed there by soldiers and left to die. Executed for having committed some heinous crime.

The man on the middle cross seems to be receiving all the attention. There's a sign hanging over his head. Soldiers stand beneath his cross, guarding him closely. Onlookers yell obscenities at him. Some people are drawing straws to see who gets to take the condemned criminal's seamless garment home for themselves. One observer even puts vinegar on a sponge and mockingly offers it to him as a drink.

The scene disturbs you. Mobs are never pretty.

You have witnessed nothing like this before, so you walk even closer, wanting to know what in the world is going on. Who are these three men? And why are people so riled up?

You ask a woman on the edge of the crowd, "What's this all about?"

"They're crucifying Jesus for being a rebel, a blasphemer. I have no idea who those other two men are," she replies.

You've heard of this man, Jesus. Some people told you he is a miracle worker. Others suggested he is a great teacher and sage. And a few people told you that he is the Son of God.

You can't look away. The scene is too compelling. So you watch these three executions. And you listen carefully to the sounds around you.

The crucified convict on the left rails at Jesus in his last moments of life on earth.

"Aren't you the Christ? Save yourself and us!" he barks desperately.

It's hard to believe one dying convict is actually berating another one, but a dying man looks for any way out.

But the second convicted criminal, the one on the right,

chooses a different approach. He recognizes he deserves the death sentence for his crimes. He possesses self-awareness. He's come to terms with his mistakes. In fact, he seems almost at peace with his circumstances.

He rebukes the convict on the left. "What are you doing? You and I are getting what we deserve for our crimes." He glances at Jesus and says, "But this man has done nothing wrong."

The criminal clearly recognizes Jesus's innocence. And yet Jesus hangs dying, crucified between two guilty convicts.

Finally, the self-aware criminal looks at Jesus, digs deep for his own humility and pleads, "Jesus, remember me when you come into your kingdom."

This man's simple words acknowledge three things:

1. The convict has done something wrong and he knows it. He is guilty. And he deserves death.
2. Jesus has done nothing wrong. An innocent man does not deserve this horrific execution. A grave injustice is taking place on that cross.
3. Jesus holds the key to forgiveness and to eternal life. Even in this dark moment, grace is still available.

And so, the convict shares his final words with Jesus: "Remember me."

Remarkably, Jesus responds, "Today you will be with me in paradise."

Eventually, the Church chose to name this repenting criminal Dismas. A good thief crucified. A man whose dying breaths ask for mercy from the only One who can give it. A repenter saved in his final hour. A man keenly aware of his sin, who turned away from it and sought new life with Jesus.

And Jesus does it. He forgives. Right then. Right there. As they die.

While He undergoes an excruciating death, subjected to the humiliation of the crowd, Jesus actually pauses and forgives. It's astonishing. He stares into the eyes of death, and rather than complaining about the pain, Jesus opens the door of forgiveness right there in front of everyone.

The self-aware criminal then steps directly into paradise.

Dismas makes the truth plain: Jesus forgives.

FORGIVENESS COACHING TIP 5:
Experience God's Forgiveness

Given the opportunity, Dismas welcomed Jesus' offer of forgiveness. The opportunity arrived, and he took it.

The sacrament of Reconciliation (Confession) provides that opportunity. Jesus stands waiting and ready to offer that same grace to you. When you welcome it, your heart will change.

Once you experience His mercy, you won't be able to help yourself. You will live differently. Free and light.

And you'll begin to see others in a fresh way, as imperfect people worthy of forgiveness, just like you.

You'll even begin to see your Somebody with new eyes. Because your heart will have been softened.

Decide today to go to Confession. Mark a day on your calendar. Experience God's forgiveness just like Dismas did.

CHAPTER 6

Forgive Yourself: Ron

*Often I wish my enemies and
those who try to hurt me an*

*equal harm, like to like—as
anger meets anger and hate*

*meets hate—but You keep
reminding me, early and late,*

that love is unlike meeting like.
— Meister Eckhart —

At age fourteen, Ron met pornography. It seemed harmless at first. He watched a video with a friend.

Of course, as a young man, he found it sexually exciting. But he never allowed himself to get sucked into the vortex of looking at pornography on a regular basis. He knew he needed to avoid the temptation. But somehow, the more he fought the temptation, the harder it was to resist.

Then, he discovered online porn, and he was hooked. He

began to rely on sexual fantasy through his phone and videos. It soon became a daily habit.

Ron's relationship with God was a "Don't call me, I'll call you" thing. When life was going well, he never even considered praying. It was only when life became difficult that he would consider asking the Lord for help.

When Ron got married, he started looking at pornography less. But after the birth of a second child, he and his wife were no longer intimate the way he longed for, for reasons he didn't understand. So, he returned to the porn habit to try to satisfy his sexual desires.

He kept videos saved on his phone and laptop where his children and wife wouldn't find them. Or so he thought.

He never talked about pornography to anyone. That part of his life he kept private, not realizing he was digging himself deeper and deeper into addiction.

This pattern continued until a single moment jarred Ron's life.

His wife and sons were away for a weekend, and he found himself home alone. First out of boredom, and then out of an inner compulsion, he voraciously consumed more and more porn. When his family returned home, Ron's four-year-old son picked up his father's phone. Somehow, a pornographic video began to play on the screen. The little boy said, "Dad, there's something really gross on your phone."

Ron's heart sank as he rushed to turn off the video. Today,

the son doesn't remember the incident, but it has scarred Ron knowing he brought evil into his home and family.

He knew he had to be strong for his wife. He set out to find the road to healing. But that road was filled with ups and downs. However, Ron found a renewed faith in Christ Jesus and learned to seek Him when he was tempted.

First, he needed to forgive himself for all the years of addiction and the stain of those images in his mind. As temptation resurfaced, Ron drew closer to Christ. He found strength by helping other men who had pornography addictions. Helping them made it easier for him to fight his own temptation. And to learn to treat himself as kindly as he treated them.

More healing arrived when Ron sat down with his wife. He confessed everything to her and asked for forgiveness. Deeply wounded and hurt, she found the grace to gently and generously give the forgiveness he craved. Their relationship began to improve.

Eventually, Ron could see the fruits of his relationship with Christ. He dove eagerly into his Catholic faith. His prayer life expanded. He grew to rely on the Blessed Mother and the saints. He joined a men's Bible study. This isn't a road to travel alone.

Having other healthy men around him has made the journey easier.

Over time, Ron began to seek out Christian men to keep him accountable to his path of faith and recovery. At meetings, men stood up and confessed their own addictions to pornography—with raw honesty and integrity. Their inspiration nourished Ron.

Finally, he realized his own sons would be tempted to look at pornography just like he had. He knew well how aggressively porn sites bombard you and lure your eyes through your phone. He also knew how quickly a young male brain will take that bait. At the right time, Ron talked to his boys about pornography. More important, he taught them how to have a good relationship with Jesus.

Ron continues to stumble on occasion. But his love for Christ Jesus is strong. His future is bright. His marriage continues to heal. And his sons will learn to follow God from their father's example.

Because he first learned how to forgive himself.

FORGIVENESS COACHING TIP 6:
Five Steps to Forgive Yourself

You and I are wonderfully imperfect. We all make mistakes. You are worthy of love, period. You are made in the image of God. You are much more than the worst thing you've ever done.

Forgiving other people, including your Somebody, will be very difficult if you cannot forgive yourself. Self-forgiveness is essential to becoming the best version of yourself.

Learning to forgive yourself requires empathy and kindness. It also means accepting that forgiveness is a choice.

Ron took multiple steps to grow into self-forgiveness in this story.

Five Steps to Help You Forgive Yourself

1. Acknowledge your mistake out loud
If you struggle to let go of a mistake, speak out loud your thoughts about it. This will allow you to begin to let go of the burden.

2. Think of each mistake as a learning experience

Each mistake holds the key to your being stronger in the future. Acknowledge what you learned from the mistake. And remind yourself you did the best you could with the tools you had at the time.

3. Have a conversation with your inner critic

Write out a conversation between yourself and your inner critic. This will help you identify the thought patterns sabotaging your ability to forgive yourself.

On one side of a piece of paper, write down what your inner critic says (this tends to be harsh, unforgiving, and irrational).

On the other side of the paper, write a self-compassionate and rational response for each thing you wrote on the first side.

4. Take your own advice

Ask yourself what you would tell your best friend if they were sharing this mistake with you. Practice telling your friend how to move on. Then, take your own advice.

5. Quit playing the soundtrack in your head

When you catch yourself playing the "I'm a bad person" soundtrack, stop. Focus instead on one positive action step.

For example, take three deep breaths, or go for a walk, or say, "I am someone who can be forgiven."

CHAPTER 7

Taste the Sweetness: Dominic

"I am blessed.
I am the child of a great king.
He is my father and my God.
The world may praise me or criticize me. It matters not.
He is with me, always at my side, guiding and protecting me.
I do not fear because I am His."
— Matthew Kelly —

I love development work. Inviting people to become the most generous version of themselves inspires me. Encouraging men and women to give a portion of their lives to a greater mission motivates me.

Sharing the life-giving joy of generosity is wonderful, meaningful work, as we invite people to join the movement to share good news with a broken, angry world and to bring the lost home into God's arms.

There's a well-known saying in fundraising: "Love people. Use money."

And even though you'll regularly be tempted to get that

backward—to love money and use people— don't ever do it.

Sometimes, I find it all too easy to do. Instead of loving people and using money, I can slip into the danger zone of using people to get money. Ministries need money to achieve their mission. They have budgets and goals, staff members to feed, electricity bills to pay. And when I'm not careful, I can ease into the mindset of getting money for ministry and forgetting the real human being I'm asking to give.

That happened with Dominic. He and I had been friends for two decades. He had been a vital and encouraging partner in ministry with me. As a successful entrepreneur and CEO of the company he'd founded, Dominic had been extraordinarily generous to the ministries I was involved in. He and I had become close friends well before his financial success came. I had helped him discover the beauty of the faith and the love of God. And he had been a caring friend to me in ways too numerous to count. He consistently prayed for me, and I did the same for him.

Yet I made a mistake with him. An anonymous donor to our ministry had offered to give one million dollars if we would find another donor to match that gift. I immediately thought of Dominic. He and his wife had given such gifts to ministries on a number of occasions. In fact, they had given that to my own ministry more than once.

My mistake was in thinking of Dominic as a source of funds first and a friend second. I was overeager to ask for that matching gift so our ministry could launch an initiative to lead young adults into the faith. It was important work.

Dominic and I met for breakfast. He shared an update on his life. I tried to listen to all the stresses he was experiencing. But in honesty, I only had one thing on my mind. The gift.

When the conversation paused, I pivoted to share what we were seeking to do and the potential matching gift from another donor. I hastily asked Dominic whether he and his wife would be willing to make that matching gift of a million dollars.

The blank stare he gave me stung like a dart entering my eye. I immediately realized I had violated my own core principle: Love people. Use money.

My heart sank. I was embarrassed and almost too ashamed to speak.

He politely declined my request, saying it was a little more than they were able to do at the moment and that they had already committed to two other projects that were taking up most of their funding abilities.

But I knew the truth: I had not really been listening when he was talking before I asked for the gift. I had not been loving enough to genuinely care about the pain he and his family were going through at the time. In fact, I had barely noticed what he had said.

After breakfast, I went home and sulked. Ashamed of myself. Disappointed in my failure to be a friend or even an attentive listener. Embarrassed I had not followed my own advice to love people and use money.

A few months passed. I worked up the nerve to invite Dominic for breakfast again. I had waited first out of shame at my own behavior, and second out of respect for the intensity of his schedule and not wanting to take too much of his time for my own goals.

When we met again, I started the conversation. "I want to apologize. I should not have made that ask of you the last time we met. I put money before friendship. And I failed even to listen to what you were telling me. Please forgive me."

Dominic smiled and gently said, "You were forgiven before you even asked. I love you and pray for you each day."

The grace of good friendship washed over me. What a beautiful gift he had given me. Mercy. Forgiveness. Grace.

And that gift of mercy was sweeter than any financial gift I could ever ask for.

FORGIVENESS COACHING TIP 7:
Simple Daily Prayer

Forgiveness can be difficult, and prayer will be your best friend on that journey.

Prayer softens your heart. Gently redirects your soul. Allows the hand of God to guide you where you need to be.

Cultivate a habit of daily prayer. If this habit is new to you, begin with just two minutes of silence a day in the presence of God. Simply sit in His presence. Be quiet. Listen.

Then grow slowly from there. Perhaps add one minute a day every week or two, and increase the divine silence in your life.

You simply cannot sit in the presence of God each day without becoming more grace-filled. Over time, this daily prayer will transform you into a more forgiving person. Guaranteed.

You might start with a prayer like this one:

Spirit of God,
At this time,

I am unable or unwilling to forgive.
I know not which.
Fill me with the wisdom of forgiveness.
Bring me to the beautiful truth
that forgiving others is part of my own healing.
Cleanse me of the poison of unforgiveness.
Shine light so I can see how unforgiveness
affects my physical, emotional, and spiritual health.
Today,
I am unwilling or unable to forgive.
I know not which.
Just give me the desire to forgive.
For I know, trust, and believe
that if you place the desire to forgive
firmly in my heart
that desire will grow,
and the day will come
when I am both willing and able to forgive.
Amen.
—Matthew Kelly, *Life is Messy*

CHAPTER 8

Past the Hurt: Wanda

Wanda walked into the hospital room. As a nurse, she knew something the patient did not. She knew the patient was her father. The man who had abandoned her and her sister just months after she had been born forty-one years ago. The father she had neither seen nor heard from since.

She had always wondered where her father was. The family never discussed him. No pictures. No memories. As a girl, Wanda realized that at any moment she could be standing near her father and not even realize it. She had no idea he still lived in New York City, where she and the family he had left behind also lived.

Now Wanda faced a moment of truth. As the assistant head nurse, she recognized the name of the patient, Victor. And Wanda faced a decision: how to deal with this man— first, as her long-lost father; second, as a patient nearing death from cancer.

Wanda was shaking. All the memories. All the emotions.

All the feelings of abandonment washed over her.

"I needed to go to his room," she says. "I had to see him. My mom said I resembled my dad very much. So I go into the room. He looks right at me and I realize: He looks like me and I look like him."

"Hi, how are you?" she asked. "Are you comfortable? Do you have any kids?"

"Yes, I do," he responded. "But my kids are grown. I have an older daughter Gina and a younger daughter Wanda."

At those words, Wanda rubbed her head, began to cry, and immediately left the room. Overwhelmed. It was just too much.

A few minutes later, she returned, calm. "I'm Wanda. I'm your daughter."

"I know," he said. He'd recognized the resemblance in the grown woman who looked just like him.

Victor begged for forgiveness. "I wasn't a good father."

Wanda dug deep within herself and responded, "The past is the past. You can't change it. I love you."

When Victor was moved to another room to eliminate the conflict of interest of having a family member as his nurse, Wanda introduced him to her own three children. She shared that he had five grandchildren in total. And she eventually brought her sister and her mother to meet him anew.

Then, Wanda dug still deeper. She began showing up three hours early for her shift. She sat with Victor, cared for him, shaved his beard, trimmed his nails, brought him food. She gave him a radio to listen to the classical music he enjoyed. Then, she added time after her shift as well, a few more hours while he was asleep. She simply sat with him. To be near her father. To give the beautiful gift of presence.

Had Victor been admitted to one of the other seven units in the same hospital, Wanda never would have known he was there. But given the opportunity, she maximized the moment to bring restoration and peace where there had been only loss and pain.

As Victor lay in the hospital bed, he said, "Wanda, I have met you. I'm OK. I'm ready to die."

Abandonment had been replaced by homecoming.

FORGIVENESS COACHING TIP 8:
Embrace Grace

People often hurt others because they themselves have been hurt. And each one of us has been wounded in some way.

Clearly, Victor's past decisions had harmed Wanda. His leaving had left her to grow up without a father. And that pain wounds deeply.

Damage like that can cause us to become defensive and self-protective. We may lash out at others. We may choose to spill our hurt onto other people, or even to abuse them. When that occurs, hurting people becomes a vicious, never-ending cycle.

However, Wanda chose to reject revenge and embrace grace instead. Rather than lashing out at Victor, she opted to love. And she did so with extravagance—giving her time, her attention, her love, and her gifts to the father who had abandoned her.

Think about the wounds you carry from those who have hurt you. Be honest with yourself: Are you tempted to spill that hurt onto others so that they experience the same hurts you have received? Or do you tend to withdraw a bit, just to protect yourself from possibly being hurt again?

Consider Wanda. She resisted the temptation and chose to embrace grace.

As you think about the Somebody you need to forgive, how can you do the same?

Reflect on how you might
1. See clearly how your wounds are actually an area where God can be powerfully present in your life like Wanda did,
2. Use your pain to do good rather than harm, to become strong in your broken places, and
3. Welcome the triumph of Jesus' empty tomb.

We are Easter people.
We are a people of hope.
We are a people of homecoming.
We are people of the Resurrection.

CHAPTER 9

Reach Out: Nina

"Families are definitely the training ground for forgiveness. At some point you forgive the people in your family for being stuck together in all this weirdness, and when you can do that, you can learn to forgive anyone. . . Not forgiving someone is like drinking rat poison and expecting the rats to die."

— Anne Lamott —

Nina grew up in an alcoholic family. Her earliest memories are of her father taking her and her brother to bars. The kids played darts for hours while their dad drank. They got bored, but he just kept on drinking.

Nina's father was military, and he struggled with containing a violent rage that lived within him. Once, when Nina was playing with friends, he called her in for supper. Five-year-old Nina didn't come in fast enough, so her dad struck her with his belt.

She never asked why he beat his children because she knew never to challenge his authority. He'd beat her for that too. So she lived in fear, always stuffing her thoughts and feelings deep within.

The insults, the beatings, and the pain shaped her identity. Slowly, she came to believe she was not a good person.

Nina felt good only when she was playing sports. She excelled at basketball. Her father would come drunk to every game. And he always yelled. His mere presence embarrassed her.

When Nina left home for college, she attended a retreat. There, she heard the Lord say, "Forgive your father." She responded, "Why? Look at all he's done and all the wounds he's caused. How can I forgive him?"

God replied, "Forgive him. Otherwise, you'll never be free from his sins."

Nina embraced those words, but she had no idea where to begin. She decided to relive each hurtful event from her life. In her imagination, she became a child and invited Jesus into the scene. She revisited every event where her father had hurt her. Each time, Jesus came to her afterward, picked her up, and held her until the pain went away. He then put her down and walked over to her father and embraced him.

By the time it was over, Nina loved her father. In real life, he was still drinking. He was still abusive. He wasn't a very nice man. But now she loved him.

Eventually, Nina began to pray, "Lord, I know you don't want my dad to be a drinking alcoholic for the rest of his life. When it's the right time, let me know, and I'll do whatever I can to help him."

A few years later, she sensed the Lord's nudging: "Now is the time."

She contacted a counselor, her dad's boss, and her family. They all gathered in a hotel room to hold an intervention with her father.

The counselor guided the family as they spoke to Nina's father about the things he had done to wound them. They shared how they knew he wouldn't have done them had he been sober. They told him he needed help.

He said he couldn't get help because of his work. His boss responded that the company would cover all the costs. Eventually, her dad agreed to go to a treatment center.

When his treatment ended, he returned and never drank again. He was fifty-eight years old. Nina finally met her father as a sober man. She loved getting to know him. Her dad's sobriety freed her to ask questions, and he told her stories about his life.

Nina could now see where his hurt and anger had come from. His mother had died when he was five, and his childhood had been full of violence and fear. For the first time, his behavior started to make sense.

Slowly, Nina and her father grew closer. But she still felt like a victim. How do you overcome feeling like you're not good enough?

Then she began to read the book of Genesis and noticed

something crucial: When God created human beings, He made them in His own image. With each step of Creation, God saw what He had made and said, "What I have created is very good."

Nina learned to remind herself that she was made in the image of God Himself. Which meant she was His creation and was good, even when she didn't feel it.

Over the years, she has learned to see other people through God's eyes too. She seeks to understand the hurts of the people she meets. And realizes each one of them is made in the image of God just like she is. So she moves to forgive quickly.

When her father was suffering from cancer and Alzheimer's disease, she visited him often in the nursing home. As her dad prepared to die, Nina called her mom and siblings and told them it was time to visit in person. This was the moment to say goodbye.

Nina's oldest brother, James, had a hard time forgiving their dad. In those final moments, James went to visit him. When he walked into the room, his sister said, "Dad! James is here!" Nina's father, who had been unconscious for some time, sat up, hugged his son, and said, "I've been waiting for you to come."

Their father died later that day.

After years of turbulence, peace had finally arrived.

Because forgiveness had paved the way.

FORGIVENESS COACHING TIP 9:
Know Help is Real and Available

When she needed help, Nina reached out—for herself, for her family, and for her dad.

Asking for help requires vulnerability.

There's something powerful about being vulnerable with people you trust. Raw vulnerability shuts off fear, helping you face your pain and move forward.

When you ask for help, you often discover that opening up about your regrets leads to life-changing healing. Twelve-Step groups, like Celebrate Recovery and Alcoholics Anonymous, remind us we are only as sick as our secrets. The sacrament of Reconciliation can help you do that too. You can destroy shame by bringing it into the light.

In your own journey of forgiveness, you may realize you need additional help. A gifted pastor, counselor, or guide can teach you skills and help you learn how to heal. If you're feeling buried by the task of forgiving, reach out—*today*—and get help.

CHAPTER 10

Resurrection Faith: Melissa

*"Blessed be the God and Father of our Lord Jesus Christ, the Father
of mercies and God of all comfort, who comforts us in all our affliction,
so that we may be able to comfort those who are in any affliction, with
the comfort with which we ourselves are comforted by God.
For as we share abundantly in Christ's sufferings, so through Christ
we share abundantly in comfort too.
If we are afflicted, it is for your comfort and salvation;
and if we are comforted, it is for your comfort, which you experience
when you patiently endure the same sufferings that we suffer.
Our hope for you is unshaken; for we know that as you share in our
sufferings, you will also share in our comfort."*
— 2 Corinthians 1:3-7 —

Weighing just two pounds and fourteen ounces, Melissa lay
hooked up to wires and tubes in a neonatal intensive care
unit. But there was no anxious parent nearby, lovingly holding her tiny hand, desperately willing her to live.

Melissa's mother had left the Iowa hospital, believing the
toxic saline solution she'd been given when she was nearly
eight months pregnant had aborted her child. But the proce-

dure had failed and Melissa's mother had no idea her daughter was still alive.

The doctors who carried out the abortion in Sioux City had estimated that Melissa's mother, whose identity she has chosen to keep private, was about twenty weeks pregnant. But the fact that Melissa had survived the saline infusion led them to believe her mother had actually been thirty-one weeks along.

In the NICU, Melissa suffered respiratory distress and seizures. She was expected to have vision problems, hearing loss and developmental delays as she grew.

Three weeks after her birth, she was transferred to a hospital in Iowa City. The nurses who cared for the itty-bitty baby made her tiny clothes and colorful booties.

One nurse, Mary, even named her Katie Rose.

At three months old, Melissa left the hospital and was welcomed by Linda and Ron Ohden, a couple who had already adopted a girl, Tammy, four years older than Melissa.

The Ohdens and Mary kept in touch, exchanging Christmas cards and letters with pictures and updates on her progress.

"Mary and I began a friendship that would last for decades. It made me feel so special this nurse cared for me when no one else did," says Melissa.

Early on, the Ohdens told Melissa and her sister they were adopted.

"Tammy and I fought like sisters typically do," says Melissa. "It was during one of these explosive arguments, when I was fourteen, that she blurted out, 'At least my parents wanted me!' I ran to my adoptive parents, who told me the devastating truth—that I had indeed survived a botched abortion. They had never intended for me to know.

"My world felt like it stopped that night. I felt angry, scared, ashamed and even guilty for being alive."

Melissa then spent most of her teenage years "in great emotional pain." She developed bulimia and sought escape through sex and alcohol.

She eventually headed off to the University of South Dakota. Melissa later learned her biological mother had attended there as well.

At nineteen, she began the search for her birth family. After years of futile hunting, she came across a startling lead when she was thirty. "I knew my maternal grandparents' surname and where they had been employed, so that was a big piece of the puzzle," she says.

Melissa sent them a letter. But only her grandfather wrote back. He shared that her live birth was not the intention on the day she was born. He also made it clear she wouldn't find her birth mother through them because they were estranged from her.

That same year, Melissa requested her medical records, and a breakthrough came. The hospital administrators had forgotten to obscure her parents' names in the files. After discovering she was living in the same city as her biological father, Melissa reached out to him by letter.

"I have every reason to believe he never knew I was born. I simply told him I was alive, and that I wasn't angry or bitter. But he never responded."

Six months later, she discovered he had recently died. She then made contact with his brother. His family was aware of her existence; they had come across her letter to him after his death.

"They told me he once said 'I've done something I'm so ashamed of but I can never say what.' Knowing what I know now, I take that to mean that my mother was being forced to have an abortion and he did nothing to stop it. Perhaps he felt too much shame to respond to me; I will never really know."

Melissa gave up her hunt for a while. She married Ryan, with whom she has two daughters, Olivia and Ava. Her older daughter was born at the same hospital where Melissa survived the abortion.

Then, when she was thirty-six, her biological mother's cousin emailed her. The cousin shared that Melissa's birth parents had been childhood sweethearts who were engaged to be married when she was conceived. Her mother had always had irregular periods, so she didn't realize she was pregnant until the third trimester.

"I was told she didn't want a termination, but my grandparents didn't approve of the relationship between her and my father. That was a huge shock. I'd spent so many years thinking my mother never wanted me.

"I discovered that my birth mother, aged nineteen, had been forced into the abortion by her own mother, who was an educational nurse supervisor at the hospital," says Melissa. Worse, her own grandmother had instructed the staff to "leave the baby in the room to die."

A nurse who worked at the hospital told her about the staff member who had saved her, and her grandmother's disturbing attempts to deny her a chance at life. Melissa is alive today because a nurse heard her gasps for breath as she lay discarded as medical waste.

"I have never met the woman who took me to neonatal but she's an angel. I owe her my life," says Melissa.

Finally, after seventeen years of searching, Melissa connected with her birth mother. "We chatted for three years before we met in person. I think we were both scared of rejection."

Then Melissa suggested the two should meet. Her mother responded enthusiastically. They hugged and cried. Her birth mother whispered, "I was robbed of you."

"Through my Catholic faith I have learned to forgive," says Melissa. "It doesn't make what happened OK, but it releases you from the pain. We're all human and we all make mistakes. I have only forgiveness in my heart, for my father too and even for my grandmother."

How did Melissa do it?

In her own words: "It's been a long and painful journey from shame and anger to faith and forgiveness. But I refuse to be poisoned by bitterness—that's no way to live."

FORGIVENESS COACHING TIP 10:
Recycle Your Pain

Recycling her pain is exactly what Melissa did.

She did not allow herself to drown in the aftermath of rejection and abandonment. She took that pain and reached out to help other people experiencing the same challenges she faced. Melissa Ohden founded the Abortion Survivors Network.

She knew what it was like to feel helpless and hopeless. She resolved that no one should have to experience that kind of pain and be silenced. She has now recycled her own pain into the creation of a healing mission.

In launching the Abortion Survivors Network, Melissa hoped to create a world where failed abortions and the lives of survivors are openly discussed, and survivors and their families are supported and healed. Quite simply, Melissa's ministry extends love and forgiveness to all who are impacted by abortion.

Years ago, Celebrate Recovery was started to help people discover how to process their deepest wounds and then use their own pain to support others. Their eight steps (shared below) to recycle your pain can help you process your pain and use it for good in much the same way Melissa has done.

One reason God allows pain is to give you the opportunity to serve others. Pain can make us humble and sympathetic to the hurts of the people around us.

Who better to help someone who went bankrupt than another who has lived that pain?

Who better to help a person suffering from abuse than one who has experienced abuse also?

God never wastes a hurt. Learn from your pain. Share your lessons. God invites you to use your pain to help other people.

Be open and ready. You never know when God will place someone in your life who can benefit from your pain, your experience, and your growth. Let Him redeem your suffering.

ROAD TO RECOVERY

Realize I'm not God; I admit that I am powerless to control my tendency to do the wrong thing and that my life is unmanageable.

Blessed are the poor in spirit, for theirs is the kingdom of heaven. (Matthew 5:3)

Earnestly believe: God exists, I matter to Him, and He has the power to help me recover.

Blessed are those who mourn, for they shall be comforted. (Matthew 5:4)

Choose to commit all my life and will to Jesus Christ's care and control.

Blessed are the meek, for they shall inherit the earth. (Matthew 5:5)

Openly examine and confess my faults to myself, to God, and to someone I trust.

Blessed are the pure in heart, for they shall see God. (Matthew 5:8)

Voluntarily submit to changes God wants to make in my life and humbly ask Him to remove my character defects.

Blessed are those who hunger and thirst for righteousness, for they shall be satisfied. (Matthew 5:6)

Evaluate all my relationships. Offer forgiveness to those who have hurt me and make amends for harm I've done to others when possible, except when to do so would harm them or others.

Blessed are the merciful, for they shall obtain mercy. (Matthew 5:7)

Reserve a daily time with God for self-examination and prayer to know God and His will for my life and to gain the power to follow His will.

Yield myself to God to share this Good News with others, both by my example and my words.

Blessed are those who are persecuted for righteousness sake, for theirs is the kingdom of heaven. (Matthew 5:10)

| CHAPTER 11 |

The Air You Breathe: The Amish

On a sunny, warm October Monday, twenty-six children from Amish families walked to the West Nickel Mines School near Georgetown, Pennsylvania. The children ranged in age from six to thirteen.

Their twenty-year-old teacher, Emma, had taught there for two years. Emma's mother and sister and two of Emma's sisters-in-law were visiting the school for the day. One of the younger visitors was expecting a baby.

By 9:00 a.m., Charlie Roberts, a truck driver who picked up milk from dairy farms in the area, was loading guns, ammunition, and supplies for barricading the doors of the school into a borrowed pickup truck. He had planned his assault carefully, including leaving behind suicide notes for his family to read later that day.

He drove to an auction barn across from the school and watched as the children finished recess and went back inside the building. Shortly after 10:15 a.m., he backed the truck up to the main entrance of the school. When Emma, the teacher, came to the door, he asked if she and the students could help him find a piece of metal along the road similar to one he held in his hand. He went back to the truck and then entered the school with weapons.

Emma ran out a side door with her mother to the closest farm and called 911. Meanwhile, Roberts bound the feet of some of the girls with zip ties. Soon he forced the visitors and all the boys out of the school. One girl heard a voice say "Run," and she did, leaving ten girls inside the school.

By 10:44 a.m., state troopers were arriving on the scene. Roberts had nailed boards over the doors and had pulled down the blinds. He talked about intending to molest the girls, and said he needed to "punish some Christian girls" to settle his anger with God over the death of his daughter shortly after birth nine years earlier.

The troopers interrupted Roberts' plan.

Charlie Roberts phoned 911 at 10:55 a.m. and told the operator to clear the troopers off the property or he would kill everyone inside. One of the thirteen-year-old girls, Marian, told him to shoot her first.

At about 11:05 a.m., Roberts shot all ten girls. He fired one shotgun blast through the window at the troopers but missed. The troopers stormed the building, only to see Roberts fire one last shot into his own head.

Emergency responders had already begun arriving on the scene. They transported the victims via helicopter and emergency vehicles.

Police worked to keep out onlookers and, most importantly, the media. The Amish believe it's wrong to have their pictures taken because it violates the biblical commandment not to make a graven image. They also avoid media attention because of their desire to live peaceable quiet lives, a desire cruelly shattered on this day.

The highly efficient system of Amish word of mouth spread the terrible news. About one hundred relatives of the schoolgirls soon gathered at the farm where their teacher had phoned for help. Within sixteen hours of the shooting, families knew that five of the girls had died and the other five were seriously injured.

One law enforcement official said, "There was not one desk, not one chair, in the whole schoolroom that was not splattered with either blood or glass. There were bullet holes everywhere, everywhere."

Remarkably, the first sign of healing came from an unlikely source—the victims' own families. On the day of the shooting, a grandfather of one of the murdered Amish girls warned young relatives not to hate the killer, saying, "We must not think evil of this man." Another Amish father shared, "He had a mother and a wife and a soul and now he's standing before a just God."

The Amish moved quicky to offer grace and forgiveness to Marie Roberts, the widow of Charlie Roberts, and to Charlie's parents. They comforted the Roberts family hours after the shooting. One Amish man even held Roberts' sobbing father in his arms to console him.

Most amazingly, as Amish families were burying their daughters in the days after the shooting, some joined with other members of their community and visited the Roberts family to assure them they had no hard feelings—and to express forgiveness for Charlie, even though he was dead.

Thirty members of the Amish community then attended Roberts' funeral. And the Amish set up a charitable fund to manage five million dollars in donations to the surviving girls, even giving part of the money to Marie and her children.

Marie Roberts thanked the Amish community in an open letter.

"Your love for our family has helped to provide the healing we so desperately need," she wrote. "Gifts you've given have touched our hearts in a way no words can describe. . . Your compassion has reached beyond our family, beyond our community, and is changing our world, and for this we sincerely thank you."

Media soon picked up reactions from the broader public, many of whom were shocked the Amish community would offer forgiveness so quickly and seemingly so easily.

The Amish were in turn surprised that anyone could think

they would even question whether to forgive Charlie Roberts or his family. Forgiveness is simply in the air they breathe as a community.

The Amish people fully knew they had suffered an unimaginable loss—the lives of beautiful, young, hope-filled girls. But their culture doesn't think like the world thinks.

Grace and mercy are deeply embedded in the Amish DNA. Their moral code is like a stool with three legs:

1. The example of Jesus provides the first leg of the Amish moral code. Teachings such as "Turn the other cheek;" "Love your enemies. Pray and forgive them;" and "Forgive others as you wish to be forgiven" form a kind of personal test for each member of the Amish community. As does Jesus' own example, of forgiving the woman at the well, the woman caught in adultery, and even his own executioners in His Crucifixion.

2. The Amish reinforce the teaching and example of Jesus through the regular telling of their shared stories, which they remember over and over again as a community. First, there are stories from Scripture. The girls' teacher, Emma, had begun that Monday by reading them a story from Acts 4 about being devoted to the teaching of the disciples. Second are the community's powerful stories from their own history and martyrs. Take the story of Dirk Willems, a Dutch Anabaptist: When Dirk was escaping from a man hired to catch

Anabaptists, he ran across a frozen stream. The pursuer fell through the ice during the chase. Dirk turned back and pulled the man out of the frozen stream, saving his life. He was then arrested and burned at the stake in May 1569. For the Amish community, Dirk's actions provide an iconic, inspiring story of forgiveness and love for the enemy.

3. The third leg of the Amish forgiveness stool can be found in the deep ties that bind their people together. Community, not individual, comes first. In a close-knit community, harmony disappears when hostilities fester, so grudges and hurts must be addressed openly and honestly. Forgiveness keeps the poison of bitterness from creeping into the community.

When you are Amish, the decision has already been made. You will forgive.

The Amish, with their shared life of following Jesus and their relational fabric of community, reinforced by the telling and retelling of stories, can imagine the possibility of forgiveness where forgiveness may seem impossible to other people.

The Amish community knows that forgiveness does not undo the tragedy. Instead, it takes a bold step toward healing and hope.

Forgiveness is not something the Amish do. It's who they are.

FORGIVENESS COACHING TIP 11:
Treasure Powerful, Sacred Stories

The Amish embrace a deeply ingrained habit of forgiveness. Sacred stories from the Bible, as well as their own treasured stories, like that of Dirk Willems, reinforce how they are a community forgiven by God and expected to forgive others.

You can draw ongoing strength for your forgiveness journey in the same way. Read, study, and retell powerful stories of forgiveness from our faith. Allow these stories to give you a deep reservoir of grace and memory to imagine possibilities for forgiveness in your life. Then you'll be prepared. You won't have to decide to forgive. It will just naturally flow from your soul.

Here are eight excellent stories to help you:

Genesis chapters 37–50
The powerful forgiveness journey of Joseph
(reflect on the remarkable words of grace he gives
his brothers in chapter 50)

Matthew 5:38–48
Powerful words from Jesus on forgiveness
in the Sermon on the Mount

Matthew 18:23–25
The parable of the unforgiving servant

Luke 23:26–43
The crucifixion of Jesus. Watch as He forgives those who
kill Him as well as the man being executed next to Him

John 8:1–11
Jesus forgives the woman caught in the act of adultery

Romans 12:9–21
Inspiring words from the apostle Paul
calling us to a higher way of life

Saint Maria Goretti
Patron saint of assault victims with
a remarkable capacity to forgive

Saint Maximilian Kolbe
A man who can teach us how to offer forgiveness
when it seems impossible

CHAPTER 12

Heroic Love: Leonella

"Modern culture does not rate forgiveness very highly.
More often it justifies resentment and revenge. . .
Unless we understand the importance of forgiveness and
practice it in our relations with others, we will never achieve inner
freedom but will always be prisoners of our own bitterness.
When we refuse to forgive someone for harm done to us, we are adding
another wrong to the first. That solves nothing at all. We are increasing
the quantity of evil in the world, which has quite enough as it is."
— Fr. Jacques Philippe —

Leonella Sgorbati. Say her name out loud. It's difficult to pronounce.

But I've memorized it. Because I hope to become like her.

Leonella served as the leader of the Consolata Missionary Sisters in Kenya, Africa. She then founded a nursing school in Somalia with the dream of providing health services and career options to young people there who could otherwise be lured into joining al-Shabab or other terrorist groups. Her nursing school's first students graduated in 2006.

Sr. Leonella deeply believed that giving young people a

chance, offering them something different, would move them to lay down their weapons. In fact, she said, "I know I could be risking my own life, but I will do it for love."

Love means you're willing to inconvenience yourself for someone else. And that's exactly what Leonella did. She knew that where there is fear, love withers.

Having secured funding for the nursing school in Somalia, Leonella then began scouting in Uganda for hospitals to train more of her students to work in difficult circumstances.

At the same time, she faced the challenge of new Islamic rules in Somalia. When one Somali leader told worshippers at his mosque, "Whoever offends our prophet Muhammad should be killed on the spot by the nearest Muslim," trouble began to stir.

And so, on Sunday, September 17, 2006, around midnight, Sr. Leonella was crossing the road from the children's hospital to enter the village where five of her Consolata sisters lived. The crossing is just thirty feet long.

Two assailants waited, hiding behind the taxis at the entrance of the hospital.

Ambush.

Sr. Leonella was shot in the thigh. When her security leader fired back, the Islamists shot and killed him. That leader, Mohamed Osman Mahamud, a Muslim father of four, died.

Leonella was then hit with two additional bullets, one

of which severed her femoral artery, causing a massive hemorrhage.

Taken quickly for medical help, she was surrounded by her religious sisters. They loved her till the end.

As she lay bleeding to death, Sr. Leonella Sgorbati spoke her final words in her native Italian: "Pardono, pardono." In English, "I forgive, I forgive."

Earlier, when Leonella had returned to Somalia, she had been fully aware of the danger surrounding her. "I know there's a bullet with my name on it," she had said then. "I don't know when it will arrive, but as long as it doesn't arrive, I will stay."

This sober awareness didn't discourage her. She knew God wanted her in Somalia.

Nothing could stop her devotion to the mission. She dedicated herself completely, sparing no effort to establish a school of nursing. To give hope and a future to a country ravaged by war.

"I can't be afraid and at the same time love. I choose to love."

After her death, the United Nations helped move her body and evacuate the other Consolata sisters from Somalia to Kenya. The sisters buried her in Nairobi, and her body is now kept in the Flora Hostel Chapel there.

"This sister, who for many years served the poor and the children in Somalia, died pronouncing the word 'forgive,'"

Pope Benedict XVI said. "This. . . shows the victory of love over hatred and evil."

Indeed. Those who opposed Sr. Leonella never had a chance. Love triumphs. Forgiveness wins.

Doing something each day can be tedious. It can grow tiresome, even monotonous. But the simple act of training each day transforms good athletes into great ones, good poets into Nobel Prize winners, and simple servants into saints. It will also transform you into a world-class forgiver.

Sr. Leonella understood that. She spent thirty-eight years in Africa, serving God humbly and loving people generously a little each day—even when it was tedious, even when she didn't want to.

Her love for God and the Somali people conquered any fear.

And in the end, her heart was transformed into something beautiful. A shrine of Love.

FORGIVENESS COACHING TIP 12:
Look for Love in Exactly the Right Place

One priest I know responds to every situation in the exact same way:

"That's wonderful! I can't wait to see how God shows you how much He loves you through this!"

Those words make perfect sense when someone comes to you and shares marvelous news about a new job, a long-anticipated pregnancy, or the success of a chemotherapy treatment.

However, that can be hard to hear when the priest says it in response to news about the death of your daughter, or your recent cancer diagnosis.

But that priest is right. And Sr. Leonella knew the same thing.

Every situation, every encounter, even every hurt or broken relationship really is an opportunity to discover the love of God in a new way. And to experience that love personally and powerfully.

St. Paul reminds us of this truth in Romans 8:

For I am sure that neither death, nor life, nor angels, nor princi-palities, nor things present, nor things to come, nor powers, nor height, nor depth, nor anything else in all creation, will be able to separate us from the love of God in Christ Jesus our Lord.

Write these words down. Keep them near you. Draw strength from them when your road to forgiveness gets tough.

And learn to say with the priest:

"That's wonderful! I can't wait to see how God shows you how much He loves you through this!"

You really have no idea how much God loves you.

Today Is Your Day

"Blessed are the merciful, for they shall obtain mercy."
— Jesus —

Think about Abraham Lincoln.

In 1865, the Civil War was nearing its end. This awful, violent, hate-filled four year struggle had resulted in carnage we can only begin to imagine. More than six hundred thousand men had died.

Many Northerners wanted the South to pay a heavy price as revenge for having engaged in such a bloody war in the first place.

As America turned to the reconstruction of our nation, people in the North wanted to hear from President Lincoln. They wanted answers to their questions.

"Will you allow the Southern states back into the union they left?"

"Will you make them pay, and make them pay heavily?"

"How will you exact revenge on the rebellious Southerners, Mr. Lincoln?"

To these questions, Abraham Lincoln replied, "I will treat them as if they never left."

Forgiveness. Yes, Lincoln responded with forgiveness.

How does that happen? How could President Lincoln possibly forgive the South?

Lincoln valued healing and wholeness more than punishment and revenge. He knew that was what the nation needed most. Only forgiveness could lead the United States forward. He chose forgiveness for himself and for the country.

Like Lincoln, you can choose healing. You can move toward a better, brighter future in your own life. You can forgive your Somebody. Begin with these steps:

Practice forgiveness.
Begin with the little things.
Reread and treasure these stories.
Use the coaching tips provided here.
Display forgiveness quotes.
Find new ones of your own.
Seek inspiration.
Practice forgiveness some more.

Watch, then, as you slowly and confidently become the person you desire to be. Released from the past. And moving forward.

Even better, you will know you are becoming exactly who God wants you to be: the-best-version-of-yourself.

Do not delay.
Today is your day.
Begin now.

Dr. Allen Hunt

"Yesterday is gone. Tomorrow has not yet come. We have only today."
— Mother Teresa —

Allen Hunt writes and speaks. He leads and creates. His work inspires and motivates.

While serving as a megachurch pastor, Allen began a remarkable journey culminating in his conversion to Catholicism. He now partners with Matthew Kelly to help lead the Dynamic Catholic Institute, an organization inspiring millions of Catholics and their parishes.

An author of a number of bestselling books, Allen is also a powerful speaker. His messages inspire everyday people to more fully recognize the genius and relevance of Catholicism, the role it's meant to play in their lives, and how to share this with others.

Prior to full-time ministry, Allen worked in management

consulting with Kurt Salmon Associates, an international leader in the textile, apparel, and retail industries. He was educated at Mercer University (BBA) and Emory University (MDiv), before earning a PhD in New Testament and Ancient Christian Origins from Yale University.

Allen's personal interests include hiking, literature, spirituality, history, and good food. He and his wife, Anita, live in Georgia. They have two daughters, SarahAnn and Griffin Elizabeth, two sons-in-law, and seven grandchildren.

For additional information, please visit www.drallenhunt.com.

Session One

Reading: Prologue, Introduction and Chapter 1
Opening Prayer
Discussion Questions:

- In the prologue, we meet Brian, who is carrying around a duffel bag full of grudges and resentment. What grudges and resentment are you carrying around with you every day, and what can you do today to unburden yourself of your duffel bag?
- In chapter one, Nadine Collier inspires a courtroom of grieving people to forgive a mass murderer. Who in your life inspires you to forgive, and how can you become more like that person?
- Mrs. Collier shocked the country and became famous for her words, "I forgive you." How can you shock or surprise someone with a courageous act of love today?

Closing Prayer
Announcements

Session Two

Reading: Chapters 2, 3 and 4

Opening Prayer

Discussion Questions:

- In chapter two, Allen says we learn to forgive by forgiving the little things. Recall a time in your life when forgiving a little thing prepared you to forgive a bigger thing. Or think of a time when you witnessed someone else forgiving a little thing, and what made that admirable to you.

- Sr. Therese of the Child Jesus learned to re-engineer her mindset from petty annoyance to an attitude of humble love. How would you like to reengineer your mindset? Who in your life would benefit from that re-engineering?

- In chapter three, we read about the young man who is full of bitterness and hate because of what has happened to his brother. Sometimes, it's even harder to forgive someone who has wronged a loved one than someone who has wronged us. Who might you need to forgive who has wronged someone you love?

- Who do you know who is a good forgiver? What habits do you think that person has that help make him or her a good forgiver?

- In chapter four, Allen reflects on his time serving as a volunteer at a homeless shelter where he learned that his role is not to hold God's clipboard and evaluate everyone on His behalf. What new role do you think God might be calling you to today?

- In the story of the rabbi who gives money to a struggling man, the rabbi learns that the man and his family are not struggling at all, and instead of being angry, he responds, "Thank God they are healthy!" Did the rabbi's response surprise you? If so, why? What would it take for you to be more like the rabbi in the story? What is holding you back?

Closing Prayer

Announcements

Session Three

Reading: Chapters 5 and 6
Opening Prayer
Discussion Questions:

- In chapter five, St. Dismas recognizes that he needs Jesus' mercy. In what area of your life do you need to ask Jesus for mercy, or simply accept the mercy that He has already extended to you?

- In chapter six, Ron starts his own healing process when he forgives himself. From there, more healing follows. What do you need to forgive yourself for today?

- More healing arrives for Ron when he asks for forgiveness from his wife. Is there anyone in your life you need to ask for forgiveness today? When and how will you initiate that conversation?

- Ron reflects that his pornography addiction "isn't a road to travel alone." How does this sentiment apply to your own life? What road might you be trying to travel alone that is meant to be traveled with supportive companions?

Closing Prayer

Announcements

Session Four

Reading: Chapters 7 and 8
Opening Prayer
Discussion Questions:

- In chapter seven, Dominic quickly extends forgiveness and mercy to Allen. Recall a time in your own life when someone has extended mercy or forgiveness to you. What impact did that have on you?
- In chapter eight, Wanda meets the father who abandoned her when she was a baby. Her father begged for her forgiveness, and Wanda extended mercy and love to him. Has anyone ever asked for your forgiveness? Were you able to extend it? What made it difficult?
- Wanda extended the gift of forgiveness to her father, and he was able to die in peace because of that gift. Who can you extend a little bit of peace to today, and how will you do that?

Closing Prayer
Announcements

Session Five

Reading: Chapters 9, 10 and 11
Opening Prayer
Discussion Questions:

- In chapter nine, Nina comes to believe she is not a good person. She makes her pain her identity. What might you be making part of your identity that is hurting you? What's an unhealthy part of your identity in the past that you've been able to let go of? What did that look like?

- Nina is able to love and forgive her father even when he is still drinking, still abusive and not a very nice man. Have you ever forgiven someone even though they hadn't changed their hurtful behavior? What did that look like? What made it difficult?

- Although she has forgiven her father, Nina still has to regularly remind herself that she is good enough, and that she is created in the image and likeness of God. What regular reminders do you need to set for yourself so that you can see yourself as God sees you?

- In chapter ten, Melissa, an abortion survivor, is kept alive and loved by a team of nurses when no one else wants her. Who are some people who have cared for you in various stages of your life? What did that mean to you?

- Have you ever recycled your pain to serve someone else who was hurting? What did that look like? How has God used pain from your past to help others?

- What area of pain have you not yet given to God? Are you ready to say, "God, I want you to use this pain to bring benefit to others"?

- Who in your life is a good example of using one's pain to help others?

- Letting go of grudges has deep roots in the Amish DNA. They seek to emulate Jesus Himself. How can you set an example in your own family to let go of grudges so you can start sinking deep roots and create a culture of forgiveness in your home? How would this change your family?

Closing Prayer

Announcements

Session Six

Reading: Chapter 12 and Closing Word
Opening Prayer
Discussion Questions:

- In chapter twelve, Sr. Leonella dies forgiving her assailants. Forgiveness is her legacy, and in 2018, she was beatified by Pope Francis. What do you want your legacy to be? How can you become more like Sr. Leonella today?

- Abraham Lincoln knew who he was: a forgiver. Would you describe yourself as a forgiver? If not, who is one person you can forgive today to start taking on your new identity as a forgiver?

- Throughout the book, Allen encourages his readers to practice forgiveness through twelve coaching tips. Which coaching tip did you feel most drawn to and why? What lesson are you most excited to apply to your life today?

Closing Prayer
Announcements

Acknowledgments

All of the stories contained in this book are true. In some cases, names and details have been modified in order to preserve the privacy of the individuals involved.

Gratitude for inspiration is due in the following stories:

Know Who You Are is inspired in part by Peggy Noonan's reflections on this story.

Draw Near to Forgivers is inspired in part by a reflection from Heather King.

Forgive Yourself and *Reach Out* are adapted from *Faith: The Magazine of the Diocese of Salina.*

Past the Hurt is adapted from news accounts of this story.

Resurrection Faith is adapted from *You Carried Me: A Daughter's Memoir,* by Melissa Ohden.

The Air You Breathe is adapted from several accounts of this story, including those of the Associated Press and Jeff Bach, and the book *Amish Grace* by Donald B. Kraybill, Steven M. Nolt, and David L. Weaver-Zercher.

| ALSO BY DR. ALLEN HUNT |

Confessions of a Mega Church Pastor

Dreams For Your Grandchild

Everybody Needs to Forgive Somebody

Genesis

Life's Greatest Lesson

Nine Words

No Regrets

The 21 Undeniable Secrets of Marriage

The Fourth Quarter of Your Life

The Turning Point